JEFF MANION
with Christine M. Anderson

Satisfied

Discovering Contentment
in a World of Consumption

W9-ARU-971

ZONDERVAN®

ZONDERVAN

Satisfied Study Guide
Copyright © 2013 by Jeff Manion

This title is also available as a Zondervan ebook. Visit www.zondervan.com/ebooks.

Requests for information should be addressed to:
Zondervan, *Grand Rapids, Michigan* 49530

ISBN 978-0-310-69454-0

Published in association with the literary agency of Wolgemuth & Associates, Inc.

Cover design: *Dual Identity*
Cover photography: *Shutterstock®*
Interior design: *Matthew Van Zomeren*

Printed in the United States of America

13 14 15 16 17 18 19 20 21 22 /QG/ 20 19 18 17 16 15 14 13 12 11 10 9 8 7 6 5 4 3 2 1

Contents

How to Use This Guide

Group Size

The *Satisfied* video study is designed to be experienced in a group setting such as a Bible study, Sunday school class, or any small group gathering. To ensure everyone has enough time to participate in discussions, it is recommended that large groups break up into smaller groups of four to six people each.

Materials Needed

Each participant should have his or her own study guide, which includes notes for video segments and discussion questions, as well as personal studies (including a weekly hands-on project) to deepen learning between sessions.

Timing

The time notations—for example (17 minutes)—indicate the *actual* time of video segments and the *suggested* times for each activity or discussion. For example:

> ## Individual Activity: What I Want to Remember (2 minutes)

Adhering to the suggested times will enable you to complete each session in one hour. If you have a longer meeting, you may wish to allow more time for discussion and prayer. You may also opt to devote two meetings rather than one to each session. In addition to allowing discussions to be more spacious, this has the added advantage of allowing group members to read related chapters in the *Satisfied* book and to complete the personal study between meetings. In the second meeting, devote the time allotted for watching the video to discussing group members' projects, insights, and questions from their reading and personal study.

Facilitation

Each group should appoint a facilitator who is responsible for starting the video and for keeping track of time during discussions. Facilitators may also read questions aloud and monitor discussions, prompting participants to respond and ensuring that everyone has the opportunity to participate.

Personal Studies

Maximize the impact of the curriculum with additional study between group sessions. Every personal study includes a project to complete before the next group meeting, plus reflection questions, Bible study, and a guided prayer activity. You'll get the most out of this study by setting aside about thirty to forty-five minutes between sessions for personal study, as well as additional time to complete the weekly project. Quotations throughout the personal study are from the *Satisfied* book.

The School of Contentment

Being content is perhaps no less easy than playing the violin well: and requires no less practice.

Alain de Botton

Welcome (5 minutes)

Welcome to Session 1 of *Satisfied*. If this is your first time together as a group, take a moment to introduce yourselves to each other before watching the video. Then let's begin!

Video: The School of Contentment (14 minutes)

Play the video segment for Session 1. As you watch, use the outline provided to follow along or to take additional notes on anything that stands out to you.

Notes

Most of the time, we are unaware of the mountain of things we accumulate. It takes a moving van or a fire truck to help us come to grips with the mass of our acquisition.

The teachings of Jesus are piercing:

"Be on your guard against all kinds of greed; life does not consist in an abundance of possessions" (Luke 12:15).

"For where your treasure is, there your heart will be also" (Matthew 6:21).

Questions we have to ask:

* As one who allegedly follows Christ, what claims does Jesus have on my wallet?

* What does it mean to think "Christianly" about the stuff that fills my garage, my closet, and my basement?

* How does the one I call "Lord" intend to reshape the way I view earning, spending, saving, giving, and accumulating?

"Godliness with contentment is great gain. For we brought nothing into the world, and we can take nothing out of it. But if we have food and clothing, we will be content with that" (1 Timothy 6:6–8).

The voice of contentment says, "I'm okay with it and I'm okay without it. I would like it, it would be nice, but I do not need it in order to be whole."

Contentment is having a heart that is alive to God and the people around us even when we don't have what we want.

"I have learned to be content whatever the circumstances" (Philippians 4:11).

We have to *learn* contentment—enroll in the school of contentment—and most of us will have to enroll more than once in different seasons of life.

"I can do all this through him who gives me strength" (Philippians 4:13). Paul makes this statement in the context of living the contented life.

This week's project: Count your shoes and your shirts. Give away something of value.*

Group Discussion (39 minutes)

Talk about what you just watched.

1. What part of the teaching had the most impact on you?

Mountains of Stuff

2. Jeff described three categories of stuff we typically surround ourselves with:

   ☐ *Items of frequent use*: a microwave, a bed, a coat, etc.
   ☐ *Keepsakes*: a yearbook, family photos, a dish set passed down from a grandmother, etc.
   ☐ *Other stuff*: items no longer used

   • If you used these categories to assess your current possessions, what percentage would you assign to each? For example, 30 percent for items of frequent use, 15 percent for keepsakes, 55 percent for other stuff.

---

* See the Session 1 personal study for additional guidance in completing this week's project.

- If you were to wake up tomorrow and everything you categorized as "other stuff" had somehow disappeared, would you be more likely to feel a sense of relief or a sense of loss? Why?

3. As followers of Christ, one of the key questions we have to ask is, "What does it mean to think 'Christianly' about the stuff that fills my closet, my garage, my basement?" Listed below are four verses that illustrate aspects of Christian teaching on possessions. Go around the group and have a different person read each of the verses aloud. As the verses are read, underline any words or phrases that stand out to you.

Sell your possessions and give to the poor. Provide purses for yourselves that will not wear out, a treasure in heaven that will never fail, where no thief comes near and no moth destroys. (Luke 12:33)

All the believers were united in heart and mind. And they felt that what they owned was not their own, so they shared everything they had. (Acts 4:32 NLT)

If I gave everything I have to the poor and even sacrificed my body, I could boast about it; but if I didn't love others, I would have gained nothing. (1 Corinthians 13:3 NLT)

Remember how you ... cheerfully accepted the seizure of your possessions, knowing that you have a far greater and more enduring possession. (Hebrews 10:34 The Voice)

- We sometimes tend to avoid verses about money and possessions because they make us feel uncomfortable or even guilty. But as you consider these passages, what, if anything, intrigues you or stirs within you a desire for what the verses describe?

- Based on these verses, what three or four characteristics would you say best describe the heart of a person who thinks "Christianly" about his or her possessions?

  Giving
  Sharing
  Loving

- Which of the heart characteristics do you need most? Why?

Learning Contentment

4. Contentment is not something we are born with. In describing his own experience, the apostle Paul wrote:

> I have *learned* to be content whatever the circumstances. I know what it is to be in need, and I know what it is to have plenty. I have *learned* the secret of being content in any and every situation, whether well fed or hungry, whether living

in plenty or in want. I can do all this through him who gives me strength. (Philippians 4:11b–13, emphasis added)

When Paul says he has "learned," the Greek word he uses is *manthanō* (man-than'-o). It means to acquire a habit, or to learn by practice or experience. It is the same word used in the gospel of Matthew when Jesus says, "Take my yoke upon you and *learn* from me" (Matthew 11:29a, emphasis added).

- If contentment is a satisfied heart, what do you think it means in practical terms to *learn* contentment?

- Learning something new sometimes requires *un*learning—letting go of existing perspectives or habits. What kinds of things might you have to unlearn as you begin to learn more about contentment?

- Paul makes a subtle but noteworthy distinction when he states he has learned to be content in "any" particular situation and in "every" or all situations.* Which would you say is most challenging for you right now: being content in a specific situation in

* Homer A. Kent, Jr., *The Expositor's Bible Commentary*, vol. 11, Frank E. Gaebelein, gen. ed. (Grand Rapids: Zondervan, 1978), 154.

your life, or being content in your life as a whole? What factors make it especially difficult for you?

5. Jeff pointed out that we will have to enroll in the school of contentment more than once in different seasons of life.

- Briefly describe one of your first experiences of learning contentment. What season of life were you in? What was it you chose to do without?

- What similarities and differences are there between that earlier experience and a challenge you face in learning contentment in your current season of life?

We Are Not Alone

6. In the Philippians 4 passage, the Greek word Paul uses for "content" is *autarkēs* (ow-tar'-kace). It is the source of the English word "autarky," which is a self-sufficient country that has no need for imports or economic aid. The ancient Greeks used *autarkēs* to describe a self-sufficient person. When Paul uses the word, he adds a twist by locating the source of his sufficiency not in himself but in Christ: "I can do all this through him who gives me strength."*

- Paul might have said, "I can do all this through him who gives me ... *hope*," or *peace*, or *patience*, or *self-control*. Instead, he claims Christ's *strength*. Why do you think practicing contentment specifically requires divine strength?

- As you anticipate learning about contentment and practicing it throughout this study, in what ways are you especially aware of a need for Christ to be with you and give you strength?

---

* Homer A. Kent, Jr., *The Expositor's Bible Commentary*, vol. 11, Frank E. Gaebelein, gen. ed. (Grand Rapids: Zondervan, 1978), 156.

Individual Activity: What I Want to Remember
(2 minutes)

Complete this activity on your own.

1. Briefly review the outline and any notes you took.
2. In the space below, write down the most significant thing you gained in this session—from the teaching, activities, or discussions.

What I want to remember from this session ...

Closing Prayer

Close your time together with prayer.

An Important Word about the Personal Studies

Each personal study in this guide begins with a weekly project. The project is listed first for two reasons:

1. It will require some intentionality to complete, so reading the instructions right away will help you to plan accordingly. (Saving it until an hour before the next group meeting won't do!)
2. Small groups that have field tested *Satisfied* consider the weekly projects one of the most rewarding parts of the study. At the beginning of Sessions 2–6, you'll have an opportunity to talk about how your weekly project went, so we encourage you to prioritize it even if you don't always have time to do the reading or reflection.

Session 1 Personal Study

This Week's Project

This week's project includes two actions to help you begin to practice contentment:

1. *Count your shoes and your shirts.* Include regular shoes and specialty shoes (such as golf cleats or water shoes). Include shirts, T-shirts, athletic wear, and sweaters. You can use the charts on the following page to help you assess the different kinds of shoes and shirts you own, or simply write the total number at the bottom of the charts.

2. *Give away something of value.* Find something in your home you haven't used for a while and give it to someone who could really use it or enjoy it. Examples: an ice cream maker, golf clubs, a bike rack, an extra set of dishes.

After completing each part of the project, use the space provided below or a journal to reflect on your experience. For example:

- What thoughts or feelings were you aware of as you were counting your shoes and shirts, or when you saw the totals?

- What was it like to give away something of value? Was it harder or easier than you anticipated?

Satisfied Study Guide

Shoes	Quantity
Dress shoes/heels/special occasion	
Loafers/Oxfords/boat shoes	
Boots (dress, casual, hiking, etc.)	
Sport/workout shoes	
Sneakers	
Sandals/flip-flops	
Flats	
Clogs/mules	
Slippers	
Other:	
TOTAL	

Shirts, Tops, Sweaters	Quantity
Dress shirts/blouses	
Sweaters (pullovers, cardigans, wraps)	
Sweatshirts/hoodies	
Athletic shirts/jerseys	
Sleeveless shirts (tank tops, camisoles, etc.)	
Polo shirts and Henleys	
T-shirts (long- and short-sleeved)	
Uniform/work shirts	
Other:	
TOTAL	

Read and Learn

Read the introduction and chapters 1–4 of the book *Satisfied*. Use the space below to note any insights or questions you want to bring to the next group session.

Study and Reflect

[We must] recognize the spiritual devastation that occurs when we fail to harness the power of contentment. The quest to fill the empty space with stuff is not simply illusive but can be self-destroying.

Satisfied, *page 45*

1. The goal of the *Satisfied* study is to begin a journey (or deepen the journey you're already on) toward a lifestyle of contentment and generosity. To get a feel for your starting point on this journey, use the ten questions that follow to briefly assess where you are right now. For each statement, circle the number on the continuum that best describes your response.

   a. I tend to use credit cards to buy things I can't afford.

   1 — 2 — 3 — 4 — 5 — 6 — 7 — 8 — 9 — 10

Not at all true of me	*Moderately true of me*	*Completely true of me*

   b. I often find myself thinking about what other people have that I don't.

   1 — 2 — 3 — 4 — 5 — 6 — 7 — 8 — 9 — 10

Not at all true of me	*Moderately true of me*	*Completely true of me*

c. I tend to equate my self-worth with my net worth or my possessions.

1 — 2 — 3 — 4 — 5 — 6 — 7 — 8 — 9 — 10

| Not at all true of me | Moderately true of me | Completely true of me |

d. Buying something new makes me feel better about myself.

1 — 2 — 3 — 4 — 5 — 6 — 7 — 8 — 9 — 10

| Not at all true of me | Moderately true of me | Completely true of me |

e. My ability to be content is largely dependent on my finances and/or my circumstances.

1 — 2 — 3 — 4 — 5 — 6 — 7 — 8 — 9 — 10

| Not at all true of me | Moderately true of me | Completely true of me |

f. I do not regularly give a percentage of my income to the church and/or charitable causes.

1 — 2 — 3 — 4 — 5 — 6 — 7 — 8 — 9 — 10

| Not at all true of me | Moderately true of me | Completely true of me |

g. My salary has grown in recent years, but my level of giving has not.

1 — 2 — 3 — 4 — 5 — 6 — 7 — 8 — 9 — 10

| Not at all true of me | Moderately true of me | Completely true of me |

h. My faith does not factor into my purchasing decisions. I tend to buy on impulse or rely on my own best judgment.

1 — 2 — 3 — 4 — 5 — 6 — 7 — 8 — 9 — 10

| Not at all true of me | Moderately true of me | Completely true of me |

8

The School of Contentment

i. I tend to shop when I am lonely, bored, or depressed.

1 — 2 — 3 — 4 — 5 — 6 — 7 — 8 — 9 — 10

Not at all   *Moderately*   *Completely*
true of me   *true of me*   *true of me*

j. I sometimes wonder if I will ever be able to feel content with what I have or what I earn.

1 — 2 — 3 — 4 — 5 — 6 — 7 — 8 — 9 — 10

Not at all   *Moderately*   *Completely*
true of me   *true of me*   *true of me*

Now, transfer the numbers you circled for each of the ten questions to the blanks below. Add all ten numbers and write the total in the space provided. Divide the total by 10 to identify your overall contentment score. (See example.)

Example

My Responses

a. 2
b. 4
c. 3
d. 7
e. 8
f. 1
g. 9
h. 9
i. 4
j. 7
TOTAL 54

54 ÷ 10 = 5.4

My total   My contentment score

Example

My Responses

a. _____
b. _____
c. _____
d. _____
e. _____
f. _____
g. _____
h. _____
i. _____
j. _____
TOTAL _____

_____ ÷ 10 = _____

My total   My contentment score

Finally, plot your contentment score on the continuum below by marking it with an ✗. For example, an ✗ between 5 and 6 would represent the 5.4 score from the example.

1 — 2 — 3 — 4 — 5 — 6 — 7 — 8 — 9 — 10

I'm completely content.　　　*I'm sometimes content and some-times discontent.*　　　*I'm completely discontent.*

2. What is your initial response to your overall contentment score? For example, in what ways does it seem accurate or inaccurate to you?

3. Briefly review your responses to the ten questions and circle one that you rated closest to 10. What specifically do you struggle with in this area? What makes it especially hard for you right now?

4. Take a moment to think about any changes you might want to experience throughout this study, perhaps in connection with the areas in which you struggle most with lack of contentment. One way to think about this is to consider what you would like your new "normal" to be. For example:

   I would like it to be normal that ...

I don't have to buy something new to feel better about myself.

I don't spend so much time obsessing about things I want but don't have.

I could be generous in giving to my church and charitable causes I believe in.

Complete the sentence starter below to identify two or three areas in which you hope to experience change.

I would like it to be normal that ...

What intrigues you or concerns you about taking steps to make changes in these areas?

Contentment is not achieved through getting everything we want but by training the heart to experience full joy and deep peace even when we don't have what we want.

Satisfied, page 26

Guided Prayer

Lord, I am so grateful for your goodness to me. You have been lavish with so many good gifts to me, some of which I know I have failed to recognize or taken for granted.

As I begin to learn more about practicing contentment, I feel especially challenged by ... This is hard for me because ...

I believe you may be prompting me to ... What I need most from you now is ...

I want my life to be a reflection of your generous love for me—this day and every day. Change me, Lord, and give me courage to live a life of radical contentment and trust in you. Amen.

Comparison

Envy is sorrow for another's good.
St. Thomas Aquinas, Summa Theologica

Group Discussion: Checking In (15 minutes)

A key part of getting to know God better is sharing your journey with others. Before watching the video, check in with each other about your experiences since the last session. For example:

- What was your experience of last week's project (counting shoes/shirts and giving away something of value)? What did it reveal about you? How did it challenge your thinking about contentment?

- What insights did you discover in the personal study or in the chapters you read from the book *Satisfied*?

- How did the last session impact your daily life or your relationship with God?

Video: Comparison (18 minutes)

Play the video segment for Session 2. As you watch, use the outline provided to follow along or to take additional notes on anything that stands out to you.

Notes

Comparison rarely focuses on what we have. It focuses on what somebody else has and, in comparison, what we lack.

Comparison is the enemy of the satisfied, generous life.

Jesus told a story of the owner of a vineyard and the people that he hires to work for him (Matthew 20:1–16).

"For the kingdom of heaven is like a landowner who went out early in the morning to hire workers for his vineyard" (Matthew 20:1).

The wounded rage occurred not because the twelve-hour guys had received too little but because the one-hour guys received too much. This is the problem of living by comparison.

Comparison is that wounded voice that demands, "Why them and not me?"

Whatever you purchase, somebody around you is going to get something newer, faster, or larger.

Focusing on what's in somebody else's bowl can blind us to the blessings that are in our own.

What blessings has God heaped into your bowl?

Is it possible for you to sense his nearness and to learn to love God for himself and not simply for his gifts?

God is with you even when you have been emptied out. He is with you and he is enough.

This week's project: Make a list of all the blessings in your life, everything from people and material items to spiritual blessings you enjoy.*

Group Discussion (25 minutes)

Talk about what you just watched.

1. What part of the teaching had the most impact on you?

Robbed

2. Jeff tells the story of a young couple who quickly went from gratitude to resentment when they compared their humble starter home to the elaborate home owned by friends.

---

* See the Session 2 personal study for additional guidance in completing this week's project.

- Briefly describe a past experience when comparison quickly took you from gratitude to dissatisfaction or even resentment. What was it you had but then no longer felt grateful for or enjoyed in comparison to what someone else had?

- If comparison is a thief, how would you describe what it stole from you in the situation you just described?

- How did this experience impact your relationship with God? For example, did it cause you to question God's goodness or fairness? Make it more difficult to pray or express gratitude?

The Enemy of a Satisfied Life

3. In the parable of the workers in the vineyard, the twelve-hour workers grumbled against the landowner, claiming he was not fair:

   "These who were hired last worked only one hour," they said, "and you have made them equal to us who have borne the burden of the work and the heat of the day." (Matthew 20:12)

On the face of it, this appears to be a legitimate cause for protest. But the vineyard owner cuts through the façade of their complaints and names the heart disorder that drives them:

> I am not being unfair to you, friend. Didn't you agree to work for a denarius? Take your pay and go. I want to give the one who was hired last the same as I gave you. Don't I have the right to do what I want with my own money? *Or are you envious because I am generous?* (Matthew 20:13–15, emphasis added)

The vineyard workers are so caught up in the perceived rightness of their cause that they fail to see the wrongness of their hearts. Not only are they consumed by envy, they are also self-deceived by it.

- In what ways might envy have blinded the vineyard workers to reality—about themselves, their fellow workers, their circumstances, and the vineyard owner?

- Referring to the situation you described in question 2, in what ways, if any, might you have felt like the vineyard workers—caught up in the rightness of your cause or the reasonableness of your dissatisfaction? How might you have been blind to reality?

4. Earlier in the parable, a significant moment occurs that would be easy to overlook. As the twelve-hour workers witness the foreman paying the one-hour workers an extravagant wage, they are not yet envious. In fact, they are likely not only excited by what they see but also filled with admiration at the generosity of the landowner. But then everything falls apart:

> When those came who were hired first, they expected to receive more. But each one of them also received a denarius. When they received it, they began to grumble against the landowner. (Matthew 20:10–11)

Author and pastor Eugene Peterson writes that this is what happens when a distorted self-love "twists the spontaneities of admiration into calculations of envy … The impulses in us that are designed to mature into adoring love are perverted into scheming acquisition."* On a diagram, it's a process that might look something like this:

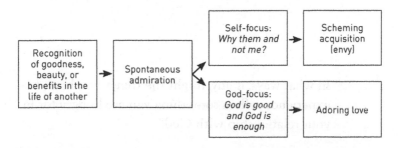

After recognizing something as good and desirable, we experience spontaneous admiration, and then we have a choice—to focus on self (through comparison) or to focus on God (through contentment).

---

* Eugene H. Peterson, *Where Your Treasure Is* (Grand Rapids: Wm. B. Eerdmans, 1993), 172.

- Generally speaking, what kinds of things do you most often find yourself "spontaneously admiring" about people recently?

- How do you imagine your life would be different if you had those things? In other words, if you look beneath the surface, what is the deeper goodness, beauty, or benefit you would hope to experience?

- In what ways, if any, might the things you hope to experience reflect something you are hungry for in your relationship with God?

A Bowlful of Blessings

5. Jeff used an illustration of two brothers and bowls of ice cream to illustrate how focusing on what's in someone else's bowl can blind us to the blessings in our own.

  - In this season of your life, how would you describe the contents of your "bowl"? In other words, what blessings do you have that you might not always recognize or be aware of?

  - When hardships make it seem like our bowl of blessings is empty, Jeff taught that these are times when we can sense God's nearness more closely and discover that God is enough. In your current circumstances, where do you sense God may be inviting you to love him for himself and not simply for his gifts?

Individual Activity: What I Want to Remember
(2 minutes)

Complete this activity on your own.

1. Briefly review the outline and any notes you took.
2. In the space below, write down the most significant thing you gained in this session—from the teaching, activities, or discussions.

What I want to remember from this session ...

Closing Prayer

Close your time together with prayer.

Session 2 Personal Study

This Week's Project

This week's project is to list blessings that fill your life. Or, to use Jeff's analogy, what's in your "bowl"? Train the eye of your heart to see the goodness around you by writing it down. Use a journal or the two blank pages that follow.

Listed below are a few big categories to jumpstart your thinking, but the possibilities are infinite. Before you start, set a goal for the number of blessings you want to write down—and make it a stretch goal! For example, fifty, a hundred, or more. You may even want to split it up and write down ten to fifteen a day for the next week.

Blessing Categories

Relationships	God's provision
Food	The five senses
Health	Christian community
Work	Opportunities
Home	Possessions
Education	Technology
Utilities (electricity, gas, water, etc.)	Talents/skills
	Knowledge
Creation and natural phenomena	Life circumstances
	Healing
Spiritual gifts or growth	

As you name each blessing, challenge yourself to be specific rather than general. For example, naming a blessing in a general way might be something like "the beauty of nature." A more specific description would be, "the beautiful colors of last night's sunset," "the shady oak tree I can sit under at the park," or "the sound of the waves at the beach."

My Bowl of Blessings

Comparison

My Bowl of Blessings

Read and Learn

Read chapters 5–7 of the book *Satisfied*. Use the space below to note any insights or questions you want to bring to the next group session.

Study and Reflect

We are prone to lose our balance, not because we have received less than we deserve but because someone near us has received more than we think they deserve. The wounded voice of comparison demands, "Why them and not me?"

Satisfied, *page 67*

1. Use the two lists that follow to briefly reflect on any tendencies you may have toward comparison and envy. Check all that apply.

   People I Tend to Compare Myself To

   - ❏ Family members
   - ❏ Friends
   - ❏ Colleagues
   - ❏ Teammates/competitors
   - ❏ Other students
   - ❏ People at church
   - ❏ Teachers/mentors
   - ❏ Neighbors
   - ❏ Other parents
   - ❏ People I frequently encounter in my daily routine
   - ❏ Famous people I admire (musicians, actors, authors, etc.)
   - ❏ Other:

Comparison

Things I Tend to Envy in Others

- ☐ Clothes
- ☐ Relationships
- ☐ Electronics/gadgets/toys
- ☐ Popularity/status
- ☐ Talents
- ☐ Appearance
- ☐ Achievements
- ☐ Job
- ☐ Opportunities
- ☐ Power
- ☐ Vehicles
- ☐ Spiritual gifts
- ☐ Travel/vacations
- ☐ Home décor
- ☐ House/property
- ☐ Income
- ☐ Life circumstances
- ☐ Other:

Now, choose two items you checked (one from each list) and circle them. Use these as your focus for the questions that follow.

What is it you admire about the person(s) you tend to compare yourself with? In other words, what about them makes you sometimes wonder, "Why them and not me?"

What is it you admire about the thing(s) you tend to envy?

What is the hidden promise in the thing(s) you tend to envy? For example, an admiration for achievements might represent the promise of recognition and praise; admiration of appearance might represent the promise of love or acceptance; admiration of a house or property might represent the promise of security.

Comparison seduces us to obsess over what is withheld while blinding us to the myriad blessings God has given for our enjoyment.

Satisfied, *page 74*

2. The group discussion for this session explored how envy played out in Jesus' parable of the vineyard workers (Matthew 20:1–16). When one of the disgruntled laborers speaks up and essentially says, "Why them and not us?" the landowner replies:

> "I am not being unfair to you, friend. Didn't you agree to work for a denarius? Take your pay and go. I want to give the one who was hired last the same as I gave you. Don't I have the right to do what I want with my own money? *Or are you envious because I am generous?*" (Matthew 20:13–15, emphasis added)

The Greek words translated in this passage as "envious" are *ophthalmos poneros* (of-thal-mos' pon-ay-ros'), which can be literally translated as "evil eye" or "bad eye." Elsewhere in Scripture, Jesus draws on this same image when he says:

> Your eye is a lamp that provides light for your body. When your eye [*opththalmos*] is good, your whole body is filled with light. But when it is bad [*poneros*], your body is filled with darkness. (Luke 11:34 NLT)

Just as we associate the heart with emotions, people in Jesus' day associated the eye with understanding and knowing. Among other things, to have a "bad eye" was to have bad judgment, to lack understanding, to be incapable of seeing people and situations clearly. Left unchecked, the deceptive power of envy that blinded the disgruntled workers to the goodness and generosity of the landowner, will inevitably blind us to God's goodness in our lives.

Where do you sense you might have a "bad eye" about God when it comes to the people and things you wrote about in question 1? In other words, name the subtle doubts or resentments about God that might be hidden behind your "Why them and not me?" question. In what ways do you wonder if God has been less than generous with you in connection with the unfulfilled promise(s) you identified?

Understand something: the heart that believes God has ripped it off can justify anything. If you believe in the core of your being that God is not good, that he is holding out on you or that he is scamming you, you can rationalize any behavior.

Satisfied, *page 73*

3. Envy can deceive us into not only questioning God's goodness but also into committing and even justifying other sins in order to get what we want. Perhaps the most chilling example of this is the religious leaders who sought to have Jesus killed. The chief priests officially charged Jesus with blasphemy (Matthew 26:59–66). But Scripture records that Pontius Pilate, the Roman governor who sentenced Jesus to be crucified, "knew very well that the religious leaders had arrested Jesus out of envy" (Matthew 27:18 NLT).

   Based on your responses in question 1, where do you sense you might be vulnerable to cutting ethical corners, being unloving, or otherwise compromising your values in order to get what you want?

4. We can't eliminate the impulse to envy simply by trying very hard not to do it, but we can choose to train our hearts toward contentment. One of the ways Christians through the centuries have redirected their hearts from self to God is to routinely pray the praises of Scripture as their own.

Psalm 145, a psalm of King David, is a beautiful example of this kind of heart-training prayer.

Using *The Message* version of Psalm 145 that follows on the next two pages, read through the psalm slowly and prayerfully. Underline on the next two pages any words or phrases that stand out to you, or write notes in the margins (or a journal) about anything that comes to mind as you pray through it. Afterward, use the questions below to reflect on your experience of praying the psalm.

What thoughts or emotions were you aware of as you prayed the psalm?

In what ways, if any, did you feel your heart or your perspective shifting as you prayed?

Psalm 145 (The Message)

1 I lift you high in praise, my God, O my King!
   and I'll bless your name into eternity.

2 I'll bless you every day,
   and keep it up from now to eternity.

3 God is magnificent; he can never be praised enough.
   There are no boundaries to his greatness.

4 Generation after generation stands in awe of your work;
   each one tells stories of your mighty acts.

5 Your beauty and splendor have everyone talking;
   I compose songs on your wonders.

6 Your marvelous doings are headline news;
   I could write a book full of the details of your greatness.

7 The fame of your goodness spreads across the country;
   your righteousness is on everyone's lips.

8 God is all mercy and grace —
   not quick to anger, is rich in love.

9 God is good to one and all;
   everything he does is suffused with grace.

10-11 Creation and creatures applaud you, God;
   your holy people bless you.
They talk about the glories of your rule,
   they exclaim over your splendor,

Comparison

12 Letting the world know of your power for good,
    the lavish splendor of your kingdom.

13 Your kingdom is a kingdom eternal;
    you never get voted out of office.
God always does what he says,
    and is gracious in everything he does.

14 God gives a hand to those down on their luck,
    gives a fresh start to those ready to quit.

15 All eyes are on you, expectant;
    you give them their meals on time.

16 Generous to a fault,
    you lavish your favor on all creatures.

17 Everything God does is right —
    the trademark on all his works is love.

18 God's there, listening for all who pray,
    for all who pray and mean it.

19 He does what's best for those who fear him —
    hears them call out, and saves them.

20 God sticks by all who love him,
    but it's all over for those who don't.

21 My mouth is filled with God's praise.
    Let everything living bless him,
    bless his holy name from now to eternity!

Guided Prayer

Lord, thank you for being so extravagantly good to me. You have blessed me in so many ways I can't even name them all.

In the days ahead, I want to choose contentment and keep my heart focused on you, but it's so hard sometimes. I often struggle with comparison and envy when it comes to …

I want my eyes to be good and full of light, not blinded by envy. I am especially concerned about how envy may have impacted the way I see you, and how I might be tempted to compromise in order to get what I want. Some of the ways I've questioned your goodness to me are … I think I may be vulnerable to compromise by … I ask you to help me …

I know that every good and perfect gift, every grace and blessing I enjoy, is an extravagantly generous display of your love for me. Please help me as I seek to train my heart for contentment and gratitude. I want to love you by living a contented and generous life. Amen.

Identity Shift

Our significance, security, and even our identity do not really lie in ourselves, but in the God who created us and who can save us from ourselves.

James M. Houston, The Transforming Friendship

Group Discussion: Checking In (15 minutes)

A key part of getting to know God better is sharing your journey with others. Before watching the video, check in with each other about your experiences since the last session. For example:

- What was your experience of last week's project (making a list of your life blessings)? Was it easy or difficult to come up with a list? Read some of your list to the group.

- What insights did you discover in the personal study or in the chapters you read from the book *Satisfied*?

- How did the last session impact your daily life or your relationship with God?

Video: Identity Shift (15 minutes)

Play the video segment for Session 3. As you watch, use the outline provided to follow along or to take additional notes on anything that stands out to you.

Notes

There is a temptation to forge our identity around what we earn, what we buy, and what we own.

Jesus said, "Watch out! Be on your guard against all kinds of greed; life does not consist in an abundance of possessions" (Luke 12:15).

As Christians, we are to have an identity that is more certain than the housing market, the stock market, and the job market.

Jesus gives new life, and with that new life he gives a new identity.

When Paul leaves Ephesus, the new Christians there were not fully formed spiritually. They had new hearts, but with old habits.

- In the first three chapters of Ephesians, Paul talks about identity; then he spends three chapters on behavior change.
- Paul uses the imagery of adoption to reach a culture known for child abandonment.
- Paul's message: *Your most defining reality is not who threw you out, but who took you in—not the parent who abandoned you, but the God who adopted you.*

This reality of adoption has the ability to reshape every aspect of life, including what we own, what we need, what we think we need.

Fred Rogers said, "The older I get, the more I've come to believe that nothing I buy can take away my loneliness, fill my emptiness, or heal my brokenness."

What this means: I don't get my identity from my car; I bring my identity to my car. I don't get my identity from my house or my career; I bring my identity to my house and my career.

Your new identity is based on *who* you belong to, and not on *what* belongs to you.

This week's project: Go on a seven-day spending fast. Enjoy the things you already have.*

Group Discussion (28 minutes)

Talk about what you just watched.

1. What part of the teaching had the most impact on you?

Identity Markers

2. Jeff pointed out that there is a temptation to forge our identities around what we *earn* (high or low), what we *buy*, and what we *own*. Using the prompts that follow, consider what each of these areas might reveal about who you are and what's important to you.

   - *What I earn.* This applies whether or not you are paid for your work. For example, if you do not earn an income, it might reveal that you are a stay-at-home

---

* See the Session 3 personal study for additional guidance in completing this week's project.

parent, retired, or have experienced unemployment. What significance (positive or negative) do you attach to what you earn? What does it reveal about who you are or who you want to be?

- *What I buy.* Consider smaller, routine purchases (such as a daily latte, smartphone apps, beauty/grooming products, eating out) as well as larger purchases (anything over $200). Focusing on a recent purchase, share what motivated your purchase and how/why you made your choice. In what ways might this purchase reveal something about who you are and what's important to you?

- *What I own.* Again, consider a range of items— books, hobby materials/equipment, clothing, electronics, furniture/decor, vehicles, house, property, etc. If someone you just met were to visit your home or ride in your vehicle, what kinds of things (positive or negative) might your possessions communicate about who you are and what's important to you?

3. When we identify with something or someone, we make a connection between ourselves and that item or person. This is a normal part of human experience. The problem comes when we *overidentify* with those things. For example, Jeff's friend Tony overidentified with having very nice new things; to not have them was not just to lose possessions but to lose a significant part of himself.

- Drawing on your responses to question 2, what kinds of things do you think you might be in danger of overidentifying with?

- What parts of your identity might be at risk if you were to lose those things?

Adopted Identity

4. Before addressing the behavior problems in the Ephesian church, Paul devotes the first half of his letter to identity — reminding his readers that they belong to God. One of the strong images Paul uses is that of adoption:

> For he chose us in him before the creation of the world to be holy and blameless in his sight. In love he predestined us for adoption to sonship through Jesus Christ, in accordance with his pleasure and will. (Ephesians 1:4–5)

To understand more about the context for Paul's statement, go around the group and have a different person read aloud each of the bullet points listed in the box titled "A Few Facts about Adoption in Ancient Roman Culture," beginning on the next page. As the list is read, underline any words or phrases that stand out to you.

- How do these facts about adoption in Paul's day impact your understanding of what it means that we are chosen and adopted by God?

- The promise of adoption would have been an especially powerful image for Paul's readers who had been abandoned at birth and were now or had once been slaves. Their identity was no longer defined by the parent who threw them out, but by the God who took them in. How does the promise of adoption impact you? In what ways do you find it meaningful—or struggle to find it meaningful—in connection with your identity as a child of God?

A Few Facts about Adoption in Ancient Roman Culture

- By law, adoption was available only to the *pater familias* (father of the family). The male head of household had authority over all family property and every person within the household, including slaves and servants as well as extended family members. The *pater familias* had legal authority to put unwanted infants to death and to sell his children into slavery. Adult children remained under the authority of the father—and could not themselves become *pater familias*—as long as their father lived.

- The adoptee was typically a young adult male (mid-teens or older) with evident health and intelligence.

- The primary purpose of adoption was to acquire an heir. An affluent couple without a son—or with an estranged son—adopted in order to pass on their wealth and to continue the family line.

- A *pater familias* could adopt a member of his own class, a slave, or a freedman (former slave).

- Adoption was relatively common among wealthy and politically connected families. It was not secret or shameful and adoptees often maintained contact with their birth families.

- There were legal distinctions for different kinds of adoption. When the adoptee was a freedman, adoption conferred to him an entirely new identity in the eyes of the law. Among other things, it meant that all existing debts or obligations were cancelled. Simultaneously, all goods and property owned by the adoptee were transferred to the ownership and control of the *pater familias*.

- It was legally permissible for a *pater familias* to disinherit close relatives, but an adoptee could not be disinherited.

Sources: Hugh Lindsay, *Adoption in the Roman World* (Cambridge: Cambridge University Press, 2009); Andrew T. Lincoln, *Ephesians*, Word Biblical Commentary, Vol. 42 (Waco: Word, 1990); Sarah Julien, "Coming Home: Adoption in Ephesians and Galatians," *Quodlibet Journal*, Vol. 5:2–3, July 2003; "Adoption in Ancient Rome," en.wikipedia.org, accessed August 9, 2013.

A New Identity

5. As God's adopted sons and daughters, our new identity must reshape our relationship with what we earn, what we buy, and what we own. Jeff described the implications of this when he said, "I don't get my identity *from* my car; I bring my identity *to* my car. I don't get my identity *from* my house or my career; I bring my identity *to* my house and my career."

   Drawing again on your responses to question 2, how would you describe the differences between getting your identity *from* or bringing your identity *to* what you earn, buy, and own?

6. Take a few moments to reflect on what you've learned and experienced together in this study so far. How has learning more about contentment impacted you?

Individual Activity: What I Want to Remember
(2 minutes)

Complete this activity on your own.

1. Briefly review the outline and any notes you took.
2. In the space below, write down the most significant thing you gained in this session—from the teaching, activities, or discussions.

What I want to remember from this session ...

Closing Prayer
Close your time together with prayer.

Session 3 Personal Study

This Week's Project

The challenge this week is to go on a seven-day spending fast. Aside from essential food and medication, make no purchases. Use and enjoy what you already have—your clothes, music, electronics, books, objects in your home. The purpose of the fast is not to avoid spending money, though that is a great side benefit! The purpose of the fast is to practice contentment by taking a break from the need to shop, consume, and accumulate.

Throughout the week, if you find yourself preoccupied with trying to find a "cheat" or a work-around, refocus your attention on the purpose of the fast, which is practicing contentment. Use the space provided below or a journal to reflect on your experiences throughout the week. For example:

- What has been the most challenging thing to fast from? Why?
- What has it been like *not* to buy things you want? What thoughts or emotions has it made you aware of?

Read and Learn

Read chapters 8–10 of the book *Satisfied*. Use the space below to note any insights or questions you want to bring to the next group session.

Study and Reflect

[T]here is a strong connection between our identity and the way we view our belongings ... many of us attempt to heal the wounds of the past by overfilling our already-full homes.

Satisfied, *page 94*

1. Read the story Jeff Manion shares in the box entitled "Keeping Up Appearances." Then respond to the questions that follow.

   Tony protected himself from the pain of a difficult childhood by vowing he would never look poor again. For him, money represented security. It helped him to feel safe and protected from the poverty and ridicule he experienced as a child. Whether or not we suffered childhood hardship like Tony, money represents something personal and significant to all of us. Of the options listed below, which comes closest to describing what money represents for you?

   - *Security*: If I have enough money, I will feel safe and secure.
   - *Freedom*: If I have enough money, I will be able to do what I like.
   - *Power*: If I have enough money, I will be successful and in control.
   - *Love*: If I have enough money, I will be loved when I use it to care for others.

What connections do you recognize between the option you checked and any formative events or wounds from your past?

In order to feel safe and secure, Tony had to keep up the appearance of affluence, which ultimately led to financial ruin. In what ways has your need—for security, freedom, power, or love—impacted the way you spend money and view the significance of your possessions?

Tony anchored part of his identity to the appearance of an affluent lifestyle. When his lifestyle was at risk, his identity was at risk. If your finances and possessions were at risk, what part(s) of your identity might feel at risk? In other words, how might you feel like you could no longer be *you*?

Keeping Up Appearances

Tony confided that he and his wife, Karen, were suffocating beneath a weight of financial pressure. This was not simply a temporary setback; they faced the very real prospect of financial ruin ... Both Tony and Karen were employed and earning strong salaries. The issue, as Tony explained it, was an inability to keep spending under control. Tony confessed that the responsibility for runaway spending was overwhelmingly his fault. He felt an urgent, inner compulsion to keep up the appearance of someone who is well off. This compulsion drove not only his choice of a home but what kind of vehicles they leased, their expensive taste in clothing and restaurants, their decision to purchase a summer cottage, their desire for a country club membership, and plans for costly vacations. The sum of these commitments was enough to capsize their financial stability.

Tony had amazing clarity as to what was driving his consumptive lifestyle. He described a childhood of scarcity, shortage, and embarrassment. His father moved out when he was six, leaving his mother to support three children on an income that fell below the poverty line. One of Tony's most painful memories was being mocked by other kids in seventh grade for wearing pants that were way too short. He had experienced a growth spurt over the summer, and there was no money available to purchase clothing for the new school year. The ridicule took the form of that well-worn joke that Tony's pants were so high because he was preparing for a flood. This in turn led to the shorthand nickname "Flood" (or in some cases "Noah") — a moniker he wore throughout middle school, even after better-fitting clothes were purchased.

There were other memories — an empty refrigerator, subsidized school lunches, and his mother's constant fretting about overdue bills. But the laughter he endured over the short pants left the most indelible mark. Reliving the experience made it difficult for him to even make eye contact. As Tony shared these reflections, he stared down at his espresso cup, which rested on the table between us. Shame has a long memory.

As a seventh grader, Tony made a silent, determined vow that he would never, ever look poor again. Now sitting in front of me was a fairly successful forty-three-year-old man, strained to the breaking point financially in an attempt to fulfill that vow. Every purchasing choice was calculated to make an impression. But it seemed that no matter how much money they earned, it wasn't enough to compensate for the humiliation that had etched itself into his identity . . .

Though Tony had a great deal of clarity on what was driving his spending, he seemed powerless to alter his compulsive behavior. Keeping up the appearance of wealth had become so central to his sense of self that not spending was like not breathing. To delay a purchase felt a bit like drowning. His identity, his life, depended on it.

Satisfied, *pages 85–88*

Identity as God's beloved sons and treasured daughters is the starting point for thinking clearly about who we are, what we have, and what we want.
                                                        Satisfied, *page 96*

2. Keeping in mind your responses to question 1, use the two-page chart that follows to locate the need you identified. Read through the associated Scriptures and underline any words or phrases that stand out to you for whatever reason. Then respond to the questions below.

   The passages you just read provide a biblical perspective on a need you associate to some degree with your money or possessions. In what ways, if any, did the passages you read challenge you about or shed light on your relationship with money and possessions?

   If your finances and possessions were at risk, what truths do these passages contain to combat the idea that your identity is also at risk?

What I Need	Scripture
Security	In peace I will lie down and sleep, for you alone, LORD, make me dwell in safety. (Psalm 4:8)
	God's a safe-house for the battered, a sanctuary during bad times. The moment you arrive, you relax; you're never sorry you knocked. (Psalm 9:9–10 MSG)
	The LORD is my strength and my shield; my heart trusts in him, and he helps me. (Psalm 28:7)
	How great is the goodness you have stored up for those who fear you. You lavish it on those who come to you for protection, blessing them before the watching world. (Psalm 31:19 NLT)
	God guards you from every evil, he guards your very life. He guards you when you leave and when you return, he guards you now, he guards you always. (Psalm 121:7–8 MSG)
	The Lord can be trusted to make you strong and protect you from harm. (2 Thessalonians 3:3 CEV)
Freedom	I have gained perfect freedom by following your teachings. (Psalm 119:45 CEV)
	Jesus replied, "I tell you the truth, everyone who sins is a slave of sin. A slave is not a permanent member of the family, but a son is part of the family forever. So if the Son sets you free, you are truly free." (John 8:34–36 NLT)
	As long as you did what you felt like doing, ignoring God, you didn't have to bother with right thinking or right living, or right anything for that matter. But do you call that a free life? What did you get out of it? Nothing you're proud of now. Where did it get you? A dead end. (Romans 6:20–21 MSG)
	Now the Lord is the Spirit, and where the Spirit of the Lord is, there is freedom. (2 Corinthians 3:17)
	For you have been called to live in freedom, my brothers and sisters. But don't use your freedom to satisfy your sinful nature. Instead, use your freedom to serve one another in love. (Galatians 5:13 NLT)

cont.

What I Need	Scripture
Power	Only through God can we be successful. It is God alone who will defeat our enemies and bring us victory! (Psalm 60:12 The Voice) *Look, does it make sense to truly become successful, but then to hand over your very soul? What is your soul really worth? (Matthew 16:26 The Voice)* Lay yourself bare, facedown to the ground, in humility before the Lord; and he will lift your head so you can stand tall. (James 4:10 The Voice) *Be strong in the Lord and in his mighty power. (Ephesians 6:10)* Do nothing out of selfish ambition or vain conceit. Rather, in humility value others above yourselves, not looking to your own interests but each of you to the interests of the others. (Philippians 2:3–4)
Love	Love your enemies! Pray for those who persecute you! In that way, you will be acting as true children of your Father in heaven. (Matthew 5:44–45 NLT) *When I was hungry, you gave me something to eat, and when I was thirsty, you gave me something to drink. When I was a stranger, you welcomed me, and when I was naked, you gave me clothes to wear. When I was sick, you took care of me, and when I was in jail, you visited me. (Matthew 25:35–36 CEV)* Those who accept my commandments and obey them are the ones who love me. (John 14:21 NLT) *We are many parts of one body, and we all belong to each other. (Romans 12:5 NLT)* Be joyful. Grow to maturity. Encourage each other. Live in harmony and peace. Then the God of love and peace will be with you. (2 Corinthians 13:11 NLT) *Most of all, love each other as if your life depended on it. Love makes up for practically anything. (1 Peter 4:8 MSG)*

It is from a conscious decision to live out of our new identity, our sense of belonging, that true life-change is possible.

Satisfied, *page 90*

3. Jeff's friend Tony understood what drove his spending, but he felt powerless to change. As you reflect on your responses in this session, what issues or behaviors are you aware of that you wish you could change? In other words, how do you sense God may be inviting you to live out of your new identity in this area of your life?

Guided Prayer

Lord, thank you for adopting me and giving me a new identity as your child. I want the truth that I belong to you to change me from the inside out so that it impacts every area of my life.

When it comes to money and possessions, I am struggling with … This is hard for me because …

I know that living out of my new identity will require that I make some changes in the way I think about and use money. Please change my heart in connection with … I especially need your power and strength to help me with …

God, I am your child and I want that to be the identity that defines me. Please help me this week especially to bring my true identity to everything I have and everything I want. Hold me secure and help me to remember that because I belong to you, I already have everything I need. Amen.

SESSION 04

The Challenge of Affluence

The most important commandment of the Judeo-Christian tradition is to treasure God and his realm more than anything else.

Dallas Willard, The Divine Conspiracy

Group Discussion: Checking In (15 minutes)

A key part of getting to know God better is sharing your journey with others. Before watching the video, check in with each other about your experiences since the last session. For example:

- What was your experience of last week's project (going on a spending fast)? What did the fast reveal to you about your typical spending habits? What did you learn or become aware of during the fast that you want to incorporate into your life now that the fast is over?

- What insights did you discover in the personal study or in the chapters you read from the book *Satisfied*?

- How did the last session impact your daily life or your relationship with God?

Video: The Challenge of Affluence (15 minutes)

Play the video segment for Session 4. As you watch, use the outline provided to follow along or to take additional notes on anything that stands out to you.

Notes

What do you enjoy and where do you experience the pleasure and presence of God in those enjoyments?

The challenge: How to have hope in God and not the things we accumulate. *The question*: Do God's gifts stir up or eclipse our affection for the Giver?

Paul gave Timothy specialized instructions for the financially well off:

"Command those who are rich in this present world not to be arrogant nor to put their hope in wealth, which is so uncertain, but to put their hope in God, who richly provides us with everything for our enjoyment" (1 Timothy 6:17).

Enjoy your house, enjoy your clothes, enjoy your food; just don't put your hope in them.

How can the heart continually move upward with worship and gratitude, but not hold God in contempt by loving his gifts more than loving him?

"Command them to do good, to be rich in good deeds, and to be generous and willing to share. In this way they will lay up treasure for themselves as a firm foundation for the coming age, so that they may take hold of the life that is truly life" (1 Timothy 6:18–19).

We overcome arrogance, self-importance, and greed not by thinking about ourselves less, but by thinking of others more.

Servanthood:
A major hurdle to a life of goodness is that good isn't good enough; we want to do something great. As we wait to do something great, opportunities to do something good go marching by.

What if we arrive at greatness through doing good things over and over again? What if greatness is goodness compounded?

Generosity:
Most people spend first; and if there is money left over, they save; and then if there is money left over, they give. Those who are generous reorder their lives so they can give first, then save, then spend. They set their standard of living after setting their standard of giving.

Hear God say, "Enjoy the thousands of blessings I send your way, but don't put your hope in your stuff. Serve and share."

This week's project: Serve somewhere you don't normally serve.*

Group Discussion (28 minutes)

Talk about what you just watched.

1. What part of the teaching had the most impact on you?

Enjoying Gifts, Loving the Giver

2. Jeff talked about how he loves to ride his bike to a coffee shop where he can sit and read or write in his journal. In enjoying moments like this, he senses God whispering, "Enjoy this. Enjoy this as a gift from my hand."

   What would you say are your equivalents to the gift Jeff described—things you especially love and enjoy? For example, they might be places you love to be, or things you love to do (photography, playing an instrument, grilling with friends, etc.). Briefly identify two or three.

3. A question we have to ask ourselves is, "Do these gifts stir up or eclipse my affection for God?" Or, as Jeff put it for himself, "How can I fall more in love with God than with my bike?"

   - Of the things you identified in question 2, which one would you say most consistently stirs up your love for God and makes you aware of his goodness to you?

---

* See the Session 4 personal study for additional guidance in completing this week's project.

- Which would you say is most at risk for potentially eclipsing your love for God? In other words, you might be more attached to the gift than the Giver?

- One way to gauge our attachment to God's gifts is to ask, "How would I respond if God asked me to give up this activity, or to sell or give away this item?" What thoughts or emotions come to mind when you ask this question about the thing that is most at risk for eclipsing your love for God?

Rich Christians

4. We may not consider ourselves well off, but by global standards, the majority of North Americans are. Among other things, we are blessed with:

   ☐ Choices and opportunities
   ☐ Public education
   ☐ Access to food, clean water, and sanitation
   ☐ The ability to clothe and feed ourselves
   ☐ Access to shelter and basic protection against violence
   ☐ A system of laws protecting basic human rights and providing access to justice

   For a quick perspective on what it means that these things constitute wealth, go around the group and have a different person read through each of the bullet points in the box "Six Facts about Worldwide Poverty" on the next page. Then respond to the questions that follow.

- In light of what you just read, to what degree would you say you are routinely aware of the wealth around you? Choose a number on the continuum below that best describes your awareness, and share the reasons for your response.

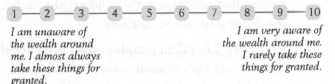

I am unaware of
the wealth around
me. I almost always
take these things for
granted.

I am very aware of
the wealth around me.
I rarely take these
things for granted.

- How do you think Christians, both those within your Christian community and others you know well, tend to define what it means to be rich? To what degree, if any, does their perspective differ from that of people you know who are not Christians?

- Overall, would you say that the Christians you know consider themselves to be rich, or is "rich" more likely to be something they feel they haven't yet achieved?

Six Facts about Worldwide Poverty

- Approximately 2.7 billion people in the world live on less than $2 a day.

- Around the world, 114 million children do not get a basic education, and 584 million women are illiterate.

- Five million people, mostly children, die each year from waterborne diseases.

- More than 2.6 billion people—over 40 percent of the world's population—do not have basic sanitation.

- More than 800 million people go to bed hungry every day, and 300 million of those are children.

- In developing countries, the poor are disproportionately impacted by illegal detentions and overloaded legal systems. In India, there are eleven judges for every one million people. In the Philippines, the average judge has a backlog of 1,479 cases. Kenya has only sixty-three lawyer prosecutors for a population of 30 million.

Sources: The UN Millennium Project, "Fast Facts: The Faces of Poverty" (unmillenniumproject.org); U.N. Commission on Legal Empowerment of the Poor (undp.org); International Justice Mission (IJM.org).

5. The life to which Jesus calls his followers is one of willing self-denial—to take up a cross and lose one's life in order to find it (Matthew 16:24–25). It is to live a life marked by an ever-increasing love of God and others (Matthew 22:36–40; John 13:34–35). But wealth has the power to pull us in opposite directions, which is one of the concerns

the apostle Paul has about the affluent Christians in Ephesus. In his first letter to Timothy, he identifies some of the spiritual challenges posed by wealth and then prescribes training and instruction for those in the church who are well off:

> Command those who are rich in this present world not to be arrogant nor to put their hope in wealth, which is so uncertain, but to put their hope in God, who richly provides us with everything for our enjoyment. Command them to do good, to be rich in good deeds, and to be generous and willing to share. In this way they will lay up treasure for themselves as a firm foundation for the coming age, so that they may take hold of the life that is truly life. (1 Timothy 6:17–19)

In what subtle or not-so-subtle ways do you sometimes default to putting your hope in wealth, or to relying more on your own resources rather than God? In other words, how do you tend to expect that money or possessions will take care of you and meet your needs?

Serve and Share

6. To combat the perils of arrogance and misplaced hope, Paul encourages those who are well off not to think of themselves less but to think of others more. He reminds his readers that the mark of those who are truly wealthy is their heartfelt generosity, and he identifies four ways they can use their wealth wisely: (1) do good, (2) be rich in good deeds, (3) be generous, (4) be willing to share.

- Jeff pointed out that sometimes what prevents us from doing good is that "good" doesn't seem to be good enough; we want to do something *great*. Also, when it comes to being generous, sometimes we struggle because we put our standard of living ahead of our standard of giving. What kinds of things tend to get in the way of your ability to do good and to be generous?

- What work do you hope God might do in your heart to combat these negative tendencies?

Individual Activity: What I Want to Remember
(2 minutes)

Complete this activity on your own.

1. Briefly review the outline and any notes you took.
2. In the space below, write down the most significant thing you gained in this session—from the teaching, activities, or discussions.

What I want to remember from this session ...

Closing Prayer

Close your time together with prayer.

Session 4 Personal Study

This Week's Project

The challenge this week is to serve somewhere you don't normally serve. For example, you might volunteer to clean up after an event at church or a local 5K charity race, assist a neighbor with a cleaning project, or help someone move. For ideas, consider your responses to questions 2 and 3 of the personal study, or do some brainstorming with another person in your small group.

Part of the purpose of serving is to combat the cultural messages that try to get us to believe "It's all about me." So as you consider where to serve, try to choose something for which you will not receive a lot of attention or recognition. Quietly, humbly serve and offer your service as a gift to God. Afterward, use the space provided below or a journal to reflect on your serving experience. For example:

- What, if anything, surprised you about your serving experience?

- How did serving impact your heart and your relationship with God?

Read and Learn

Read chapters 11–13 of the book *Satisfied*. Use the space below to note any insights or questions you want to bring to the next group session.

Study and Reflect

What daily enjoyments fill your life?... We enjoy bread and cheese ... We savor the flavors of rich coffee, tangy oranges, tart apples, and crisp carrots. And he, the Creator, provides all this—intending for us to find his generous hand behind the dozens of enjoyments of each day and turn to him in gratitude.

Satisfied, *pages 117–118*

1. Living in an affluent culture, it's easy to forget that literally every good thing we have is a gift from the God who "richly provides us with everything for our enjoyment" (1 Timothy 6:17). It is God's extravagant generosity—from the goodness of creation to the gift of his only Son, and all the blessings we enjoy—that is the starting point for living a generous life.

   Before considering your experience of God's generosity, how would you describe your experience of generosity from others? Check the statement below that best describes your response.

   ❑ I have never experienced generosity from others.
   ❑ I have rarely experienced generosity from others.
   ❑ I have occasionally experienced generosity from others.
   ❑ I have frequently experienced generosity from others.
   ❑ I have very frequently experienced the generosity of others.

In what ways, if any, would you say your experiences of generosity in others have impacted your perceptions of God's generosity with you? For example, if others have been extremely generous to you, you might either experience God as similarly generous, or you could feel disappointed that God seems less than generous by comparison.

One way to assess what we really believe about God's generosity is to consider our own. If someone were to look at an unbiased report of how you use your money and possessions, what might he or she conclude about what you believe about God's generosity?

As I hear the Creator whisper, "Enjoy this," a sincere question should arise from my heart: "In response to your goodness, is there anything you desire from me?" And my Lord will likely answer, "Yes, I want you to share."
Satisfied, *page 132*

2. In the apostle Paul's instructions to the affluent Christians in Ephesus, he identifies four ways of responding to God's goodness and generosity:

> Command them to *do good*, to *be rich in good deeds*, and to *be generous* and *willing to share*. In this way they will lay up treasure for themselves as a firm foundation for the coming age, so that they may take hold of the life that is truly life. (1 Timothy 6:18–19, emphasis added)

Listed below are the four commands Paul identifies. As you read through each one, use the prompts to first consider the state of your heart. For example, do you feel resistant, eager, grudging? Write down whatever comes to mind. Then, if you have a willingness to respond, identify one or two ways you might act on the command within the next week.

Do good: Instead of indulging in things you don't really need, make positive use of your resources by using them to help someone else.

The state of my heart right now in response to this command is …

I want to respond to this command by …

Be rich in good deeds: Don't limit your generosity to writing a check. Give of yourself. Invest your heart and your time as well as your gifts and skills with people who could use your companionship as well as your help.

The state of my heart right now in response to this command is …

I want to respond to this command by ...

Be generous: Be quick to offer what you have and do so with enthusiasm—no halfhearted joyless giving!
The state of my heart right now in response to this command is ...

I want to respond to this command by ...

Be willing to share: Cultivate a heart that has a bias for sharing, always looking for opportunities to be generous.
The state of my heart right now in response to this command is ...

I want to respond to this command by ...

Giving is the natural outflow of the thankful heart. Sharing is living in step with a God whose heart is wildly generous.

Satisfied, page 133

3. In taking steps toward a more generous life, we can be tempted to think that only grand gestures or large checks count. But the promise of Scripture is that *everything* counts — God honors, multiplies, and rewards every heartfelt act of generosity (Proverbs 19:17; Luke 21:1–4; John 6:9–13; 2 Corinthians 9:6–8). Jesus spoke these encouraging words to his followers:

   > This is a large work I've called you into, but don't be overwhelmed by it. It's best to start small. Give a cool cup of water to someone who is thirsty, for instance. The smallest act of giving or receiving makes you a true apprentice. You won't lose out on a thing. (Matthew 10:42 MSG)

   Since everything counts, you can start small! Of the ideas you listed in response to question 2, what one thing are you willing to commit to doing this week?

   An apprentice is a trainee, someone who learns by working with a master. What is it you especially want to learn from Jesus about living a generous life?

Guided Prayer

Lord, thank you for all the generous gifts you have given me on this day alone—from simple pleasures to the beauty of the world around me, I believe these are all things you want me to enjoy.

Even so, I sometimes find it hard to believe, really believe, that you are generous with me. I struggle with this because ...

I know that giving and sharing begin on the inside with the state of my heart. Right now, the state of my heart is ... Please change my heart and help me to ...

God, I want my life to be rich toward you—I want to be free of my own selfishness so I can experience the joy that comes from living a generous life. I apprentice myself to you, and ask that you give me a heart that is always looking for opportunities to be generous. Amen.

The Generous Heart

Jesus, the God-Man, had infinite wealth, but if he had held on to it, we would have died in our spiritual poverty.
                    Timothy Keller, Counterfeit Gods

Group Discussion: Checking In (15 minutes)

A key part of getting to know God better is sharing your journey with others. Before watching the video, check in with each other about your experiences since the last session. For example:

- What was your experience of last week's project (serving someplace you don't normally serve)? What did you learn about the quest for contentment while serving? If you interacted with other people while serving, what was that experience like and how did it challenge you with respect to growing in contentment?

- What insights did you discover in the personal study or in the chapters you read from the book *Satisfied*?

- How did the last session impact your daily life or your relationship with God?

Video: The Generous Heart (18 minutes)

Play the video segment for Session 5. As you watch, use the outline provided to follow along or to take additional notes on anything that stands out to you.

Notes

In a materialistic, debt-ridden consumer culture, pursuing a generous lifestyle is one of the most countercultural things a person can do.

The question we have to ask: Will we have enough, and will we be enough, as we pursue a lifestyle of systematic and generous giving?

Do not underestimate the power of fear to cripple the generous life.

Growing in the art of generosity will require that we grow in the art of trusting God.

Corinth was a strategic center for commerce and trade. By the first century, Corinth had eclipsed Athens as the most important city in the region.

Paul had asked the Corinthians to assist with a famine relief offering. The Corinthians had promised their eager support, but they had not given as they promised.

In 2 Corinthians 8 and 9, Paul teaches what it means to have a truly generous heart.

- "Whoever sows sparingly will also reap sparingly, and whoever sows generously will also reap generously" (2 Corinthians 9:6).
- The farmer's dilemma: How much grain do I plant? How much do I keep to feed my family? How much do I keep in reserve for future years?
- "And God is able to bless you abundantly, so that in all things at all times, having all that you need, you will abound in every good work" (2 Corinthians 9:8).

When you give generously, you involve yourself in a cycle of trust. It's trust that God superintends a cycle of care where I give and he provides.

There is one lethal word that can paralyze generous giving, and that's the word "later." Do not become a victim to well-intentioned delay.

Begin somewhere—begin now—to set aside a portion of your income for giving.

As you pursue the generous life, you are simply responding to a generous God.

This week's project: For the next month, raise your giving by 1 percent.*

---

* See the Session 5 personal study for additional guidance in completing this week's project.

Group Discussion (25 minutes)

Talk about what you just watched.

1. What part of the teaching had the most impact on you?

The "Want-To"

2. As you watched the video and realized that in this session
   you would be talking about giving and generosity, what was
   your first thought or initial reaction? Overall, how would
   you describe your comfort level in talking about money and
   giving in connection with your faith?

3. Jeff opened the video by describing the journey John took
   from being an impulsive and nominal giver to being a systematic and generous giver. As his heart changed, he found
   himself *wanting* to reorient his financial world to put God
   first. Which of the following six statements best describes
   your "want-to" when it comes to systematic and generous
   giving? Share the reasons for your choice.

   ☐ I don't want to reorient my financial world—at least,
      not right now.
   ☐ I am willing to want to, but I'm not there yet.
   ☐ I want to, but something is holding me back.
   ☐ I want to, and I am beginning to take some steps in that
      direction.

   cont.

☐ I want to reorient my financial world (or have already done so) and am willing to do whatever it takes to follow through on my commitment.

☐ Other:

The Enemy: Fear

4. When we first begin to pursue a generous life, we enter a war zone — an internal battle in which fear is our enemy. It's a fear the writer of Hebrews understood well. After encouraging his readers to love one another through generous acts of hospitality and compassion, he writes:

> Keep your lives free from the love of money and be content with what you have, because God has said, "Never will I leave you; never will I forsake you." So we say with confidence, "The LORD is my helper; I will not be afraid. What can mere mortals do to me?" (Hebrews 13:5–6)

The words God is quoted as saying are from the Old Testament book of Deuteronomy, and the context is an impending battle. After wandering in the desert for forty years, the ancient Israelites are about to enter the Promised Land, but first they must conquer the enemy nations already living there. Moses reassures the people with these words:

> Be strong and courageous. Do not be afraid or terrified because of them, for the LORD your God goes with you; he will never leave you nor forsake you. (Deuteronomy 31:6)

• How would you describe the unnamed fear the author of Hebrews seems to be addressing? In other words, what vulnerabilities or anxieties might be hidden behind a love of money or a lack of contentment?

- In what ways do you relate to the fears you just identified?

- If pursuing the generous life begins as a battle, how would you describe the "enemy territory" you face? What resources or reassurance do you need from God in order to engage the battle?

The Cycle of Trust and Care

5. Embedded in the apostle Paul's writing to the Corinthian church is some of the most helpful material in the Bible on what it means to truly pursue the generous life. Go around the group and have a different person read each verse aloud. As the passage is read, underline any words or phrases that stand out to you.

> [6]Remember this—a farmer who plants only a few seeds will get a small crop. But the one who plants generously will get a generous crop. [7]You must each decide in your heart how much to give. And don't give reluctantly or in response to pressure. "For God loves a person who gives cheerfully."

[8]And God will generously provide all you need. Then you will always have everything you need and plenty left over to share with others. [9]As the Scriptures say,

"They share freely and give generously to the poor.
Their good deeds will be remembered forever."

[10]For God is the one who provides seed for the farmer and then bread to eat. In the same way, he will provide and increase your resources and then produce a great harvest of generosity in you. [11]Yes, you will be enriched in every way so that you can always be generous. And when we take your gifts to those who need them, they will thank God. (2 Corinthians 9:6-11 NLT)

Paul uses the farming metaphor to motivate his readers. He wants them to understand that their gifts are not losses, but participation in something much larger—a cycle of trust and divine care.

- There are at least three participants in the cycle of trust and care that Paul describes: the giver, the recipient, and God. Based on the passage, how would you describe the responsibilities of each participant? How would you describe the benefits that each receives?

- Briefly describe an experience you or someone you know has had of the divine cycle of care. For example, were you the giver or the receiver? How did the experience impact your relationship with God and your ability to trust him?

- What do you find most motivating about this passage in connection to your own desires to live a more contented and generous life?

Trusting a Generous God

6. Pursuing generosity requires trust. We trust that the God who provides us with everything we need to be generous will continue to provide for us when we give.

   - When you think about making generosity a lifestyle, what areas of your life do you tend to find it difficult to trust God with? In other words, what vulnerabilities do you fear you'll be exposed to if God doesn't come through for you?

   - If you could consistently give the way the 2 Corinthians passage describes — cheerfully and liberally — what kind of "harvests" would you hope to realize?

Individual Activity: What I Want to Remember
(2 minutes)

Complete this activity on your own.

1. Briefly review the outline and any notes you took.
2. In the space below, write down the most significant thing you gained in this session—from the teaching, activities, or discussions.

What I want to remember from this session ...

Closing Prayer

Close your time together with prayer.

Get a Head Start on the Discussion for Session 6

As part of the group discussion for Session 6, you'll have an opportunity to talk about what you've learned and experienced together throughout the *Satisfied* study. Between now and your next meeting, consider taking a few moments to review the previous sessions and identify the teaching, discussions, or insights that stand out most to you. Use the worksheet on the following pages to briefly summarize the highlights of what you've learned and experienced.

Session 6 Head Start Worksheet

Take a few moments to reflect on what you've learned and experienced throughout the *Satisfied* study. You may want to review notes from the video teaching, what you wrote down for "What I Want to Remember" at the end of each group session, responses in the personal studies, etc. Here are some questions you might consider as part of your review:

- What insights did I gain from this session?
- What was the most important thing I learned about myself in this session?
- How did I experience God's presence or leading related to this session?
- How did this session impact my relationships with the other people in the group?

Use the spaces provided below and on the next page to briefly summarize what you've learned and experienced for each session.

Session 1: The School of Contentment

Session 2: Comparison

Session 3: Identity Shift

Session 4: The Challenge of Affluence

Session 5: The Generous Heart

Session 5 Personal Study

This Week's Project

Many of us get stuck. While seeing forward movement in paying off debt, paying down a mortgage, or increasing the percentage we invest, the percentage of our giving stays the same. The challenge for this session is to get unstuck. *For one month*, commit to increasing your giving by 1 percent. If you currently give nothing consistently, give away 1 percent of your earnings this next month. If you currently give 10 percent of your income, boost it to 11 percent for a month, etc.

Use the space provided below or a journal to reflect on your experience of increasing your giving. Even if you haven't actually "written the check" yet, you can reflect on what doing so will require of you. For example:

- What potential changes did/might you have to make in your spending in order to accommodate an additional 1 percent in giving? How did/might these changes impact you?

- In what ways did/might your increased giving require you to trust God more? How did/do you sense God working on your heart in this process?

Read and Learn

Read chapters 14–16 of the book *Satisfied*. Use the space below to note any insights or questions you want to bring to the next group session.

Study and Reflect

Sacrificial giving unleashes a spiritual wrestling match ... Something in our heart is moved toward generosity, and something in our heart resists it.

Satisfied, *page 149*

1. Briefly assess your *attitudes and beliefs* related to giving by rating the degree to which you agree or disagree with the statements below. Use the following scale:

   3 = Very strongly agree
   2 = Strongly agree
   1 = Agree
   0 = Neither agree nor disagree
   -1 = Disagree
   -2 = Strongly disagree
   -3 = Very strongly disagree

   _____ a. I believe God owns everything and that I am a trustee of his resources.

   _____ b. I believe tithing (giving 10 percent of my income) is the biblical benchmark for giving.

   _____ c. I believe a Christian's first priority in spending is to support God's work.

   _____ d. I believe God is generous.

   _____ e. I believe giving should be a voluntary, joyful expression of my devotion to Christ.

_____ f. I believe giving should be systematic and generous rather than impulsive and nominal.

_____ g. I believe giving is part of what it means to store up treasures in heaven rather than on earth.

_____ h. I believe there are times when God asks us to be sacrificial in our giving.

_____ i. I believe I am created to be generous.

_____ j. I believe decisions about giving are spiritual decisions, reflecting something about my heart and my relationship with God.

Now use the same scale to assess your *practices and behaviors* related to giving. Rate the degree to which you agree or disagree with the statements below.

_____ a. My pattern of giving affirms that God owns everything and that I am a trustee of his resources.

_____ b. I tithe (give 10 percent of my income).

_____ c. My first priority in spending is to support God's work.

_____ d. My pattern of giving affirms that God is generous.

_____ e. I give as a voluntary, joyful expression of my devotion to Christ.

_____ f. My pattern of giving is systematic and generous rather than impulsive and nominal.

_____ g. My pattern of giving affirms that giving is part of what it means to store up treasures in heaven rather than on earth.

_____ h. There are times when my giving is sacrificial.

_____ i. My pattern of giving affirms that I am created to be generous.

_____ j. My pattern of giving affirms that decisions about giving are spiritual decisions, reflecting something about my heart and my relationship with God.

Satisfied Study Guide

Transfer your assessment numbers to the blank chart below. In each column, add the numbers and write the totals in the spaces provided.

My Attitudes and Beliefs	My Practices and Behaviors
a.	a.
b.	b.
c.	c.
d.	d.
e.	e.
f.	f.
g.	g.
h.	h.
i.	i.
j.	j.
Total	Total

Now, briefly review your responses. As you compare the two columns, note where the biggest gaps are between your attitudes and beliefs and your practices and behaviors (for example, where you rated your belief at 2 or 3 but the corresponding behavior at –2 or –3). Circle those items on your chart.

Noting your totals in the two columns, how would you describe the overall gap between your beliefs and your behaviors? Is it bigger or smaller than you anticipated?

What stands out most to you about the items you circled on your chart? For example, why do you think the gaps are larger here than in other areas?

2. If your chart reveals a wide gap, you're not alone. A recent study of more than 250,000 North American Christians found two big spiritual gaps between what people say they believe and how they behave: a stewardship (giving) gap and a serving gap. In other words, although their beliefs in giving and serving were very strong, their actual giving and serving fell far short of their beliefs.*

---

* Greg L. Hawkins and Cally Parkinson, *Move: What 1,000 Churches Reveal about Spiritual Growth* (Grand Rapids: Zondervan, 2011), 88–90.

Why do you think there is such a spiritual wrestling match for Christians when it comes to giving and serving? What kinds of things would you say account for the gaps?

How would you describe the something in your heart that is moved toward generosity and the something in your heart that resists it? In other words, what is your spiritual wrestling match?

The decisive question becomes, "If I give this away, what if I don't have enough for me?" Fear of not having enough can paralyze generosity. Fear wars with trust, each battling to become the dominant force in our decision making.

Satisfied, *page 164*

3. After teaching his followers about money and possessions, Jesus tells them not to worry about their needs, and reassures them that God can be trusted:

> Your heavenly Father already knows all your needs. Seek the Kingdom of God above all else, and live righteously, and he will give you everything you need. So don't worry about tomorrow, for tomorrow will bring its own worries. Today's trouble is enough for today. (Matthew 6:32–34 NLT)

For a fresh perspective on this familiar passage, read it again from *The Message*:

What I'm trying to do here is to get you to relax, to not be so preoccupied with *getting*, so you can respond to God's *giving*. People who don't know God and the way he works fuss over these things, but you know both God and how he works. Steep your life in God-reality, God-initiative, God-provisions. Don't worry about missing out. You'll find all your everyday human concerns will be met. Give your entire attention to what God is doing right now, and don't get worked up about what may or may not happen tomorrow. God will help you deal with whatever hard things come up when the time comes. (Matthew 6:32–34 MSG)

What would you say are the God-realities, God-initiatives, and God-provisions in your life right now? In other words, where do you sense God is actively at work—calling your attention to something, presenting you with experiences or opportunities, providing for you?

Part of what it means to "seek the Kingdom of God above all else" is to "give your entire attention to what God is doing right now." In what ways do your fears or concerns (including the spiritual wrestling match you identified in question 2) make it difficult for you to give your entire attention to what God is doing in your life right now?

[God] calls us from our small worlds and invites us into an adventure of trust. Listen for his voice: "Follow me and I will look after you. Just do what I'm asking you to do. Trust me in this adventure."

Satisfied, *page 177*

4. Every adventure, including a spiritual adventure, includes a certain amount of risk. But it also offers the potential for life-giving excitement and surprising discoveries—things we will never know by staying in our small worlds.

What is the trust adventure you sense God may be inviting you to consider when it comes to giving?

How do you hope God might use this adventure to bring life to you or to help you discover something new?

Guided Prayer

Lord, thank you that there is no gap between your love for me and your faithfulness to me. You are always good, always trustworthy, always there for me.

When it comes to giving, there is a gap between what I believe about giving and what I actually give. I want to take steps to close the gap, but there is a part of me that resists it because ...

I want to experience the adventure of trusting you in this area of my life. I want to feel fully alive in my relationship to you. I ask that you help me to begin by ...

God, even though it's hard for me, I do desire to seek your kingdom—to seek you—above all else. Please help me to keep my entire attention focused on what you are doing in my life right now. Give me the courage to follow you, one step at a time. Amen.

The Invitation

We can give without loving, but we cannot love without giving.
Victor Hugo, Les Miserables

For God so loved ... that he gave.
John 3:16

Group Discussion: Checking In (15 minutes)

A key part of getting to know God better is sharing your journey with others. Before watching the video, check in with each other about your experiences since the last session. For example:

- What was your experience of last week's project (increasing your giving by 1 percent)? If you've already "written the check," did this increase feel significant, scary, and/or painful? What does that reveal to you? If you have committed to the project but haven't yet "written the check," how has planning to give more impacted your spending decisions and your ability to trust God?

- What insights did you discover in the personal study or in the chapters you read from the book *Satisfied*?

- How did the last session impact your daily life or your relationship with God?

Video: The Invitation (22 minutes)

Play the video segment for Session 6. As you watch, use the outline provided to follow along or to take additional notes on anything that stands out to you.

Notes

For those of us who swim in affluence, to what particular felonies are our hearts susceptible?

Laodicea is the very image of financial self-sufficiency.

- Jesus' words to the Christians in Laodicea: "You say, 'I am rich; I have acquired wealth and do not need a thing.' But you do not realize that you are wretched, pitiful, poor, blind and naked" (Revelation 3:17).

- They were financially wealthy but spiritually bankrupt. Their affluence led not to spiritual prosperity but to spiritual decline. And it happened without them realizing it.

- Jesus said to them, "I counsel you to buy from me gold refined in the fire, so you can become rich; and white clothes to wear, so you can cover your shameful nakedness; and salve to put on your eyes, so you can see" (Revelation 3:18).

- They didn't recognize that they needed his wealth, his covering, his healing.

The Invitation

Affluence is not always a friend to faith. As wealth grows, spiritual drift often follows in its wake.

Warner Sallman's painting, *Christ at Heart's Door*, is taken from this verse: "Here I am! I stand at the door and knock. If anyone hears my voice and opens the door, I will come in and eat with that person, and they with me" (Revelation 3:20).

Jesus is addressing believers from the city of Laodicea, the church that had grown financially wealthy but was spiritually bankrupt.

Christ is knocking. It's an invitation to a church that has lost its way.

This week's project: To help you continue your journey to a satisfied, contented life, choose one of the projects from the last five sessions and continue to practice it.*

---

* See the Session 6 personal study for additional guidance in completing this week's project.

Group Discussion (21 minutes)

Talk about what you just watched.

1. What part of the teaching had the most impact on you?

Searching for Wealth

2. In describing the beginning of his marriage, Jeff said, "We had nothing." Then he went back through the story searching for signs of wealth and concluded, "By the standards of billions living in the developing world, we were wealthy then, even when we felt well below average."

   • How would you describe the standard by which you and the people you know tend to assess financial status—both your own and that of others? In other words, what attributes make someone wealthy versus poor or average?

   • How do you respond to the idea of using the living conditions in the developing world as the standard for determining relative wealth or poverty? For example, does it seem meaningful to you or is it hard to relate to? Why?

Self-Sufficiency and Spiritual Drift

3. Jeff used the church at Laodicea as an example of how
   material abundance can shift the focus of our trust from
   reliance on God to reliance on self. For the Laodiceans, this
   shift had devastating spiritual consequences:

   > You say, "I am rich; I have acquired wealth and do not need a
   > thing." But you do not realize that you are wretched, pitiful,
   > poor, blind and naked. (Revelation 3:17)

   The description of the Laodiceans' spiritual condition is
   one of extreme misery, distress, and helplessness—and they
   are blind to it.

   - Jesus' words in Revelations 3 are addressed not to
     an individual but to a church in an affluent culture.
     Knowing that they are spiritually destitute but
     collectively self-deceived about it, how do you
     imagine their condition might have impacted the
     church overall? For example, you might consider the
     way they worshiped, prayed, and studied Scripture,
     as well as their ability to grow in love for God and
     others, extend compassion, and share their faith.

   - In what ways, if any, do you recognize similar
     dynamics in your own faith community and among
     people you know (friends, family, church members,
     etc.)?

4. Financial self-sufficiency caused the Laodiceans to become spiritually stagnant—they no longer recognized their need for Christ. After describing them as spiritually "wretched, pitiful, poor, blind and naked," Jesus says to them:

> I counsel you to buy from me gold refined in the fire, so you can become rich; and white clothes to wear, so you can cover your shameful nakedness; and salve to put on your eyes, so you can see. (Revelation 3:18)

The passage uses three key metaphors to describe the remedy for the Laodiceans' bleak spiritual condition:

Gold refined in the fire. This image refers to the spiritual wealth that comes when our faith proves genuine, especially through hardships and trials (see 1 Peter 1:7).

White clothes. In contrast to the black wool for which Laodicea was famous, Christ speaks of white clothes, which are symbolic of righteousness (see Revelation 3:4; 4:4; 6:11; 7:9).

Salve to put on your eyes. To have any hope of healing, we have to first recognize and acknowledge our blindness. Jesus said, "I entered this world to render judgment—to give sight to the blind and to show those who think they see that they are blind" (John 9:39 NLT).*

- What connections or parallels do you recognize between the remedies Christ names and the spiritual condition of the Laodiceans (described in Revelations 3:17)?

---

* Robert H. Mounce, *The Book of Revelation, rev. ed.*, The New International Commentary on the New Testament, Gordon D. Fee, gen. ed. (Grand Rapids: Wm. B. Eerdmans, 1977, 1998), 111–112.

- Of the three metaphors, which would you say comes closest to representing something you want or need from Christ, perhaps especially in connection with your tendencies toward self-sufficiency?

A Beautiful Invitation

5. At the end of the video, Jeff described the Warner Sallman painting of Jesus titled *Christ at Heart's Door*. The painting is based on the words of Christ to the church of Laodicea, which had become financially wealthy but spiritually impoverished. Jesus seeks them out and extends an invitation:

  > Here I am! I stand at the door and knock. If anyone hears my voice and opens the door, I will come in and eat with that person, and they with me. (Revelation 3:20)

  - In your journey toward contentment, where is Jesus saying, "Here I am!"? In other words, what is it he might be encouraging you to pay attention to?

  - His invitation is about companionship around a shared meal in your home. How do you need Jesus to be with you right now, or to nourish you?

6. Take a few moments to discuss what you've learned and experienced together throughout the Satisfied study.

  • What would you say is the most important thing you learned or experienced? How has it impacted you (for example, in your attitudes, behaviors, relationships, etc.)?

  • How have you recognized God at work in your life through the study?

Individual Activity: What I Want to Remember
(2 minutes)
Complete this activity on your own.

  1. Briefly review the outline and any notes you took.
  2. In the space below, write down the most significant thing you gained in this session—from the teaching, activities, or discussions.

What I want to remember from this session ...

Closing Prayer
Close your time together with prayer.

Session 6 Personal Study

This Week's Project

The challenge this week is to choose a project that will help you to take the next transformative step on your journey toward a lifestyle of contentment and generosity. One way to do this is to return to one of the projects from previous sessions and continue to practice it or even to take it up a notch. Here, as a reminder, were those projects:

Session 1: Give away something of value.

Session 2: Make a list of the blessings in your life.

Session 3: Go on a spending fast.

Session 4: Serve somewhere you don't normally serve.

Session 5: Increase your giving by 1 percent.

It could also be that God may be inviting you to do something new as an act of trust. The main questions to consider are these:

- What has seized your heart?
- What practices need to continue?
- Where do you sense Jesus saying, "Here I am!"?
- What would most encourage your continued journey toward the satisfied, contented life?

Use the space provided below or a journal to reflect on any of these questions and to identify your next steps.

Read and Learn

Read chapters 17–19 of the book *Satisfied*. Use the space below to note any insights or questions you want to bring to the next group session.

Study and Reflect

Learning contentment is a lifetime journey.

Satisfied, *page 40*

1. In Session 1, you had the opportunity to assess your starting point on the journey toward a lifestyle of contentment and generosity. Having completed the *Satisfied* study, use the same assessment from Session 1 to briefly assess where you are right now. For each statement, circle the number on the continuum that best describes your response.

   a. I tend to use credit cards to buy things I can't afford.

   1 — 2 — 3 — 4 — 5 — 6 — 7 — 8 — 9 — 10

Not at all true of me	Moderately true of me	Completely true of me

   b. I often find myself thinking about what other people have that I don't.

   1 — 2 — 3 — 4 — 5 — 6 — 7 — 8 — 9 — 10

Not at all true of me	Moderately true of me	Completely true of me

   c. I tend to equate my self-worth with my net worth or my possessions.

   1 — 2 — 3 — 4 — 5 — 6 — 7 — 8 — 9 — 10

Not at all true of me	Moderately true of me	Completely true of me

   d. Buying something new makes me feel better about myself.

   1 — 2 — 3 — 4 — 5 — 6 — 7 — 8 — 9 — 10

Not at all true of me	Moderately true of me	Completely true of me

e. My ability to be content is largely dependent on my finances and/or my circumstances.

1 — 2 — 3 — 4 — 5 — 6 — 7 — 8 — 9 — 10

Not at all   *Moderately*   *Completely*
true of me   *true of me*   *true of me*

f. I do not regularly give a percentage of my income to the church and/or charitable causes.

1 — 2 — 3 — 4 — 5 — 6 — 7 — 8 — 9 — 10

Not at all   *Moderately*   *Completely*
true of me   *true of me*   *true of me*

g. My salary has grown in recent years, but my level of giving has not.

1 — 2 — 3 — 4 — 5 — 6 — 7 — 8 — 9 — 10

Not at all   *Moderately*   *Completely*
true of me   *true of me*   *true of me*

h. My faith does not factor into my purchasing decisions. I tend to buy on impulse or rely on my own best judgment.

1 — 2 — 3 — 4 — 5 — 6 — 7 — 8 — 9 — 10

Not at all   *Moderately*   *Completely*
true of me   *true of me*   *true of me*

i. I tend to shop when I am lonely, bored, or depressed.

1 — 2 — 3 — 4 — 5 — 6 — 7 — 8 — 9 — 10

Not at all   *Moderately*   *Completely*
true of me   *true of me*   *true of me*

j. I sometimes wonder if I will ever be able to feel content with what I have or what I earn.

1 — 2 — 3 — 4 — 5 — 6 — 7 — 8 — 9 — 10

Not at all   *Moderately*   *Completely*
true of me   *true of me*   *true of me*

The Invitation

Transfer the numbers you circled for each of the questions to the blank column on the left. Add all ten numbers and write the total in the space provided. Divide the total by 10 to identify your overall contentment score. Then turn back to the assessment you completed in the Session 1 personal study. Transfer your Session 1 numbers to the column on the right.

My Responses Today   **My Responses from Session 1**

a. _____   a. _____

b. _____   b. _____

c. _____   c. _____

d. _____   d. _____

e. _____   e. _____

f. _____   f. _____

g. _____   g. _____

h. _____   h. _____

i. _____   i. _____

j. _____   j. _____

TOTAL _____   TOTAL _____

_____ ÷ 10 = _____   _____ ÷ 10 = _____

My total   My contentment   My total   My contentment
            score   score

Finally, plot today's contentment score on the continuum below by marking it with an X. Then plot your contentment score from Session 1 by marking it with an O.

1 — 2 — 3 — 4 — 5 — 6 — 7 — 8 — 9 — 10

I'm completely   I'm sometimes   I'm completely
content.   content and some-   discontent
                        times discontent

2. Briefly review the results from your two assessments. As you compare the two, what stands out to you?

Contentment is the cultivation of a satisfied heart. It is the discipline of being fully alive to God and to others whatever our material circumstances.
Satisfied, *page 26*

3. Briefly review your response to question 4 in Session 1, which was about the changes you hoped to experience and what you wanted your new "normal" be in connection with contentment. What changes or progress have you experienced in moving toward your goal? Consider shifts in your heart as well as in your choices and behaviors.

Concerted effort is required to maintain spiritual devotion in the event of financial prosperity. As net worth climbs, a strong dose of self-awareness and humility are required if the heart is to move God-ward.
Satisfied, *page 185*

4. In the book of Proverbs is a prayer of a wise man named Agur. The prayer tells that Agur is a man who knows the dark corners of his own heart and yet desires more than anything to live in harmony with God.

O God, I beg two favors from you; let me have them before I die. First, help me never to tell a lie. Second, give me neither poverty nor riches! Give me just enough to satisfy my needs. For if I grow rich, I may deny you and say, "Who is the LORD?" And if I am too poor, I may steal and thus insult God's holy name. (Proverbs 30:7–9 NLT)

Agur's first request is for honesty; he wants to live a life of integrity. He knows that his natural tendency would be to drift toward deceit, and he begs God to keep him free of it.

As you consider your desire to live a more generous and contented lifestyle, where do you sense you might tend to drift toward deceit? For example, where are you prone to engage in self-deception about your finances or the state of your heart when it comes to being generous? Or, in what ways might you tend to subtly massage the truth about your giving or finances with others?

Agur's second request is for simplicity; he wants to have a modest lifestyle. Here again, he knows his heart and how extremes in his financial circumstances might cause him to drift from God.

Given your current financial circumstances, what is it that might cause you to drift from God or dishonor him?

Agur asked God to protect him from his own tendencies to drift spiritually because he so deeply desired to live in harmony with God. As you continue to take steps on your journey to contentment, what is it you desire most from God?

Guided Prayer

Lord, thank you for inviting me on this journey to a more satisfied and generous life. I know I still have so much to learn, but I am grateful for the progress I've experienced. Thank you especially for the changes I've experienced in these areas ...

I am aware of how my financial circumstances can cause me to drift spiritually. In the days ahead, I ask that you would protect me from my tendencies to ...

Lord, more than anything, I don't want to forget you. Deliver me from the illusion that my finances and my possessions are my own. Give me a wildly generous heart, one that delights to share the gifts you have so generously given to me. Help me to honor you and to love you more every day. Amen.

Satisfied

Discovering Contentment in a World of Consumption

Jeff Manion

JEFF MANION

Satisfied

Discovering Contentment
in a World of Consumption

Why does a contented, satisfied life feel so evasive? What deep hungers drive the reckless purchasing habits, out of control accumulation, and crazy consumer lifestyle for so many of us? And why are we often driven more by what our neighbors own than what will truly make us happy?

For many in the recent economic financial crisis, a series of lifestyle adjustments became necessary as hours were slashed at work and paychecks diminished. Vacations were simplified or canceled. Even important purchases had to be delayed, and any extras were put on hold.

In the midst of paring back and cutting down there lies the critical question: Will a spirit of resentment and complaint invade our heart, or can deep, inner joy prevail, even as our dreams seem to fade? Is it possible to live a deeply satisfied life as possessions and opportunities slip away?

Followers of the Christ, living in the first-century world, also wrestled with issues related to material longings. For Christians living in Ephesus, Philippi, and Laodicea, the tendency to find their identity through accumulation and comparison was alive and well. These powerful longings are addressed in numerous places in the storyline of Scripture—a storyline that points us toward material and financial sanity and the pathway to true abundance and deep satisfaction.

Satisfied will draw richly from seven passages of Scripture, exploring the way in which these messages were received by the original readers and the way these passages can transform the way we view wealth, accumulation, and ultimate contentment today.

Available in stores and online!

ZONDERVAN®
.com

The Land Between

Finding God in Difficult Transitions

Jeff Manion

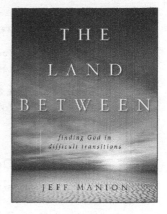

Author Jeff Manion uses the biblical story of the Israelites' journey through the Sinai desert as a metaphor for being in an undesired time of transition. After enduring generations of slavery in Egypt, the descendants of Jacob travel through the desert (the land between) toward their new home in Canaan. They crave the food of their former home in Egypt and despise their present environment. They are unable to go back and are incapable of moving forward. Their reactions provide insight and guidance on how to respond to God during our own seasons of difficult transition.

The Land Between provides fresh biblical insight for people traveling through undesired and difficult transitions such as foreclosure, unemployment, uncertainty, and failure. Such times provide our greatest opportunity for spiritual growth. God desires to meet us in our chaos and emotional upheaval, and he intends for us to encounter his goodness and provision, his hope and guidance.

A four-session DVD study with discussion questions is also ͟͟ͅͅable.

Share Your Thoughts

With the Author: Your comments will be forwarded to the author when you send them to *zauthor@zondervan.com*.

With Zondervan: Submit your review of this book by writing to *zreview@zondervan.com*.

Free Online Resources at

www.zondervan.com

Daily Bible Verses and Devotions: Enrich your life with daily Bible verses or devotions that help you start every morning focused on God. Visit www.zondervan.com/newsletters.

Free Email Publications: Sign up for newsletters on Christian living, academic resources, church ministry, fiction, children's resources, and more. Visit www.zondervan.com/newsletters.

Zondervan Bible Search: Find and compare Bible passages in a variety of translations at www.zondervanbiblesearch.com.

Other Benefits: Register to receive online benefits like coupons and special offers, or to participate in research.